A SPECIAL PLACE for SANTA

A Legend For Our Time

by
Jeanne Pieper

A SPECIAL PLACE FOR SANTA

Summary: A brief history of legends surrounding St. Nicholas, leading to his modern counterpart, Santa Claus, who pays tribute to the birth of Christ on Christmas.

1. Santa Claus–Juvenile fiction. 2. Jesus Christ–Juvenile fiction.
(1. Santa Claus–Fiction. 2. Jesus Christ–Nativity–Fiction. 3. Christmas–Fiction.)

Author: Jeanne Pieper

Illustrator: Renée Graef

Cover design by A.J.Gauer

ISBN 0-9616286-1-8

Published by: ROMAN, INC.
              555 Lawrence Ave.
              Roselle, IL 60172-1599

Third edition

Printed in USA

A SPECIAL PLACE for SANTA

A Legend For Our Time

by
Jeanne Pieper

DEDICATION

To my children—
Jerry, Tom, Peg, Greg, Mary-Beth, Mark & Judy,
To my children's children—
And to the child in everyone—
For that's what the Christmas holy-day is all about.

Raymond P. Gauer
Founder–KNEELING SANTA

INTRODUCTION
by Pat Boone

As a parent of four lovely daughters, and now a grandfather to fourteen energetic and wide-eyed grandkids, I really appreciate the message conveyed by this book.

Like you, perhaps, I've been concerned through the years with the necessity to reconcile the two major symbols of Christmas—Jesus and Santa Claus—in the thinking of my children.

How could that be done?

Children of all ages—and of all religions, or none at all—get excited about the jolly white haired gent in the red suit and black boots, because he's bringing them presents! And most of those same children have been taught by their parents and grandparents to revere the babe of Bethlehem whose birthday is celebrated on Christmas day. How can these two beloved personages be fitted together—and should they be?

When I first saw a KNEELING SANTA figurine it struck such a responsive chord in me that I wrote a song about it called, "I Saw Santa Praying." In that song—inspired by the book, "Santa and the Christ Child," previously published by Ray Gauer's KNEELING SANTA company—the dilemma is resolved. Santa Claus and Jesus of Bethlehem **do** belong together.

This narrative further strengthens that relationship by blending imagination and historical facts in a delightful way that brings Santa Claus—St. Nicholas—to his knees before the living Jesus.

May it help us all more fully appreciate the glorious fact that Christmas is the birthday of the Lord!

Once upon a time, not very long ago, two women shoppers were talking—obviously very concerned. "Buying Christmas gifts for family and friends is one thing—and I am glad to do it—but I'm afraid Santa Claus is taking over. He is causing many people to forget the real significance of Christmas."

"I agree! After all, it is Jesus' birthday!" her friend responded.

Now Santa overhears a lot when he is out making his list of who's been naughty or nice—and much of what he hears goes in one ear and out the other. But this Christmas he couldn't stop thinking about what the women had said.

Even while helping the elves load his sleigh on Christmas Eve those awful words rang in his ears. Could they possibly be right?

As he went from house to house delivering toys, Santa couldn't stop worrying. Some people *do* forget Jesus on Christmas. Could it be his fault?

Santa's last stop—as usual—was at a church that had a lifesize Nativity scene. Every year Santa loved to be the first person to wish Jesus "Happy Birthday"—and he always brought a special present for the Christ Child.

But this year Santa's footsteps were slow and heavy. He opened the door at the back of the church and crept into the very last pew. His feet refused to carry him forward to the crib where the figure of the infant Jesus lay.

He hid his present under the pew. He had never felt so drained. A tear rolled down his cheek. Even though children had left him cookies and milk – and many loving letters – he still couldn't remember when he had felt so sad or so alone.

"What's wrong? Giving presents was always such a joy before," Santa thought out loud. He sat back and closed his eyes, when suddenly he heard a voice calling, "Santa! St. Nicholas!"

Santa quickly wiped his eyes. He didn't want anyone to see him crying!

He looked around the church. The voice sounded familiar, but there was no one in sight.

"Cheer up! It's certainly not your fault that some people forget the significance of this day," the Voice continued. "Ever since you were born in far off Turkey, only 300 years after my son Jesus was born, you've done far more than most to spread the true Christmas spirit!"

Santa could hardly believe his ears. God was actually talking to him! And his voice was warm and loving. He didn't sound angry at all!

"Don't ever forget your long and distinguished career!" God continued. "It all began when, at a very young age, you were named Bishop of Myra because of your many acts of charity."

Santa smiled, suddenly remembering his colorful past. "Everyone called me Nicholas then," he recalled, "and that's when I first discovered how great it feels to help those in need."

"And you certainly helped them often," God added. "Remember that poor merchant who didn't have enough money to pay for weddings for his three daughters? You secretly threw a bag of gold into each girl's window, thinking that no one would see you—but someone did. For that good deed you were named patron saint of young marriageable maidens. The three gold balls that hang outside pawn shops to this day represent those three bags of gold."

Santa chuckled quietly. He'd forgotten that!

"You've always loved children," God reminded him, "Among many other good deeds, you were credited with rescuing some young boys from a horrible death and were named patron saint of children."

"That's the title I treasure most of all," Santa admitted.

"Well, don't tell that to the many sailors who pray to you for help when they are threatened with stormy seas or shipwreck. You are their patron saint as well!"

"And I'm the patron saint of Russia, too!" Santa added proudly. A big smile lit up his face. He certainly had led a busy and exciting life! "Churches in many cities are named after me. My feast day, St. Nicholas day, is December 6th, a very special day for celebrations and gift giving in many parts of the world."

"You are known by many names as well." God reminded Santa. "From the German you are called 'Kris Kringle', which literally means 'Christ Child.' "

"That's true—but my most popular name is Santa Claus!" Santa interrupted. "Some say it comes from the Dutch 'Sinter Claes' but I like to think it comes from the way small children say 'St. Nicholas.' '*Saint*Nicholas, *Saint*nicholas, Santa Claus!' "

Santa pulled thoughtfully on his beard and looked down at his bright red suit. Red had been his favorite color ever since he wore the red robes of a bishop. But he hadn't been so fat then!

Actually he has only had his round belly for a relatively short time. In 1823 when his friend, Clement Moore, wrote the famous poem *The Night Before Christmas*, it depicted Santa as having a round little belly that "shook when he laughed like a bowl full of jelly." Soon many people were drawing pictures of Santa.

The famous political cartoonist, Thomas Nast—who created the Republican elephant and the Democratic donkey—was one of the first to draw him with a long white beard and round belly. Later The Coca Cola Company featured a jolly Santa Claus in their Christmas advertisements. Since then, with the help of television, magazines and newspapers, the figure of Santa Claus is now known everywhere!

"Jesus and I want to thank you for helping spread the news about Christmas to every corner of the world," God said softly. "Every year you help millions of people, young and old, show how much they love one another. Because of you people everywhere fill their hearts with joy and love on Jesus' special day!"

"Thank you, God," Santa whispered. He felt better than he had felt for months. His was a very special job after all!

Santa jumped up. Next year he would work even harder filling hearts with love and joy so they would be ready for the Christ Child on Christmas morning. He could hardly wait!

The morning sun streamed through the stained glass windows of the church. It bathed the figure of the infant Jesus—and Mary and Joseph—in its bright, warm rays. Santa reached under the pew and pulled out the present he he had brought for the Christ Child.

He knew he would have to hurry if he wanted to be the first person to wish Jesus "Happy Birthday." He almost ran up the aisle—took off his hat—and knelt before the infant Jesus. He reverently placed his beautifully wrapped package next to the manger.

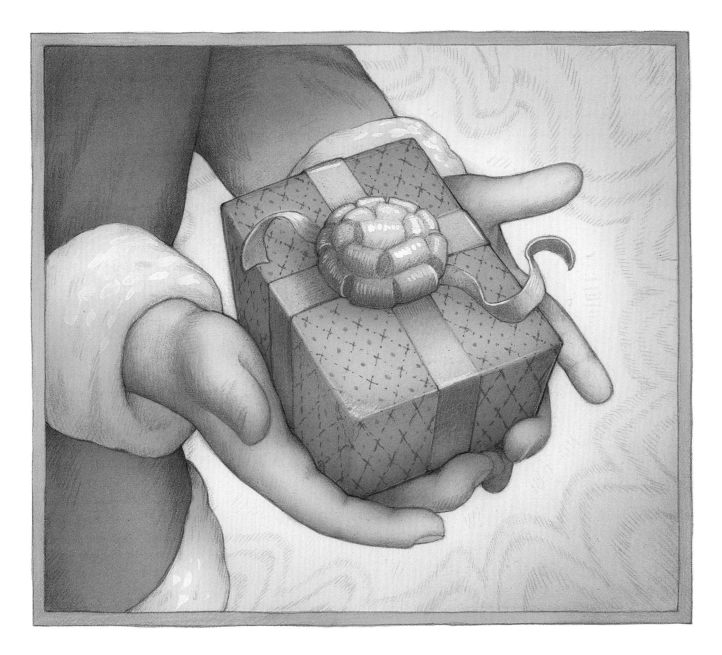

It was the same present he had given Jesus every year, but now he knew for sure it was the one present Jesus wanted most of all. Inside the box were Santa's lists of the kind and loving things people–young and old–had done for one another during the year.

"Happy Birthday," Santa whispered to Jesus. "And please thank your Father for making a special place for me in his plan. I promise never to doubt his wisdom again."

He smiled lovingly at the figure of the tiny Infant.

Now no one who comes to church on Christmas and sees Santa kneeling there thinks it strange at all. They can see that it is the perfect place for Santa Claus to be on Christmas.

And some people, the legend says, even insist that the Babe in the manger is smiling back at Santa.

About the Author:

Jeanne Pieper writes for readers of all ages–from her award winning filmstrip series for children, *"Feelings Just Are,"* produced by Franciscan Communications, to *"Seeds of Hope,"* a documentary about Indian cooperatives in Ecuador which has won a U.S. "Golden Eagle" and the "Silver Screen Award" for 1991.

A Phi Beta Kappa graduate of the University of Southern California, she lives in Malibu, has four young-adult children, and assists her husband with their family Marketing and Promotion firm.

About the Illustrator:

Renée Graef has a degree in art from the University of Wisconsin in Madison and has her studio in Milwaukee. In addition to a wide variety of commercial art, she has illustrated fourteen children's books. She has also designed a line of cloth dolls that are being marketed nationally.

Renée and her husband are expecting their first child in January, 1992.

THE KNEELING SANTA

Combining the two major symbols of Christmas—the Christ Child and Santa Claus—in a way that connotes their proper relationship—the secular subservient to the sacred—is an idea that goes back many years with Ray Gauer. While raising his own large family he became increasingly concerned about the over-commercialization of the holy day. To depict Santa Claus—St. Nicholas—on his knees before the newborn Christ Child, seemed a most effective means to counteract that trend.

The idea—which he humbly considers inspired—reached fruition in the beautiful figurine of the KNEELING SANTA which he commissioned the internationally renowned sculptor, Rudolph Vargas, to create in 1976. It has evolved into an extensive line of related products that have won a place of honor in Christian homes, schools and churches.

Raymond P. Gauer
Founder–KNEELING SANTA

©Copyright

Published by

ROMAN, INC.
555 Lawrence Ave. Roselle, IL 60172-1599